SCHOLASTIC
LITERATURE GUIDE
GRADES 4–8

Roll of Thunder, Hear My Cry

by

Mildred D. Taylor

Scholastic, Inc., grants teachers permission to photocopy the activity pages from this book for classroom use. No other part of this publication may be reproduced in whole or in part, or stored in a retrieval system, or transmitted in any form or by any means, electronic, mechanical, photocopying, recording, or otherwise, without written permission of the publisher. For information regarding permission, write to Scholastic, Inc., 555 Broadway, New York, NY 10012.

Written by Linda Ward Beech
Cover design by Vincent Ceci and Jaime Lucero
Interior design by Grafica, Inc.
Original cover and interior design by Drew Hires
Interior illustrations by Mona Mark
Photo research by Sarah Longacre

Photo acknowledgments:
Cover: From ROLL OF THUNDER, HEAR MY CRY by Mildred D. Taylor, Puffin cover illustration by Max Ginsburg. Copyright © 1991 by Max Ginsburg, cover illustration. Used by permission of Puffin Books, a division of Penguin Books USA Inc. Author photo on page 4 by Jack Ackerman courtesy of Penguin Books.

Table of Contents

Before Reading the Book

SUMMARY

The year is 1933 in the heart of the Depression. Cassie Logan and her family live in rural Mississippi, where they own and farm 400 acres. Although Cassie and her brothers attend a school for black children, she is unaware of the intense racial hatred and prejudice that exists in the community. As the story unfolds, Cassie is surprised and angered to learn that many white people think she and other black people are inferior. She learns to fear the violence that often accompanies these ugly feelings. Cassie knows how much the Logans value their land and how determined they are not to lose it. Slowly, she becomes aware of how high a price she and her family must pay to fight injustice—and to hold on to not only their land but the independence that it represents.

CHARACTERS

People

Cassie Logan ....Main character
Stacey Logan ....Cassie's older brother
Christopher-John
Logan ....Cassie's younger brother
Clayton Chester (Little Man)
Logan...................Cassie's youngest brother
Mama
(Mary Logan) ....Logan children's mother
Papa (David Logan)..Logan children's father
Big Ma (Caroline Logan)......Grandmother of
Logan children
Uncle Hammer ....Papa's older brother
Mr. L.T. Morrison ....Friend who lives
with Logans
T.J. Avery..............................Stacey's friend
Claude Avery ..............T.J.'s younger brother
Joe & Fannie Avery.......Avery boys' parents
Mr. & Mrs. Silas Lanier ....Neighbors
Jeremy Simms.........................Neighbor boy
Lillian Jean Simms........Jeremy's older sister
R.W. & Melvin Simms ....Jeremy's older
brothers
Mr. Charlie Simms.................Jeremy's father
Mr. Wellever.......................School principal
Mary Lou Wellever ....Principal's daughter
Gracey Pearson,
Alma Scott ....Cassie's classmates

Miss Daisy Crocker ....Cassie's teacher
Clarence, Moe Turner,
Little Willie Wiggins ....Stacey's classmates
Mr. Turner................................Moe's father
Mr. Harlan..........Large landowner; neighbor
Filmore Granger ....Logans' neighbor
Harrison, Montier ...Other plantation owners
John Henry Berry ....Neighbor who is
burned to death
Miss Claire Thompson ....Neighbor
Beacon Berry ....John Henry's brother
Samuel Berry ....John Henry's uncle
Mrs. Berry ....Wife of Samuel
Henrietta Toggins........Relative of the Berrys
Kaleb, Thurston, &
Dewberry Wallace ....Store owners
Ted Grimes ....Bus driver
Mr. Sam Tatum ....Man who is tarred
and feathered
Mr. & Mrs. Jim Lee Barnett.......Store owners
Wade W. Jamison ....Logans' friend/lawyer
Joe Higgins ....Banker

Animals

Lady ....Logans' horse
Jason ....Logans' hound dog
Jack ....Logans' mule

3

ABOUT THE AUTHOR

Mildred D. Taylor was born in Jackson, Mississippi, in 1943. She grew up in Toledo, Ohio, however, and graduated from the University of Toledo. Taylor then joined the Peace Corps and spent two years in Ethiopia. After her return to the United States, she entered the School of Journalism at the University of Colorado, where she was instrumental in setting up a Black Studies program. Taylor's first book about the Logan family, *Song of the Trees*, won a contest sponsored by the Council on Interracial Books for Children. *Roll of Thunder, Hear My Cry* won the Newbery Medal in 1977.

LITERATURE CONNECTIONS

Other books for young readers by Mildred D. Taylor include:
- *Song of the Trees*
- *Let the Circle Be Unbroken*
- *The Friendship*
- *The Gold Cadillac*

VOCABULARY

After presenting these vocabulary words to students, have them make a chart like the one shown below. Ask them to list each word in the first column. Then students should think about their familiarity with each word and make a check in the appropriate column. If they can define the word, they should write the definition in the next column. Once the charts are completed, invite those who can define a word to do so for the rest of the class. Challenge these volunteers to use the words in sentences.

Then direct students who did not previously check the second column to write the word's meaning in that column. After reviewing all the words, encourage students to go back and circle in red any words that they are still not sure of.

VOCABULARY FROM THE STORY

Word	I can define it.	I can use it.	I'm not sure.	I don't know it.
meticulous				
ashen				
disposition				
dubious				

meticulously	penchant	verandah	morosely
dubious	obnoxious	raucous	fallow
careened	exasperation	despondently	chignon
acrid	ashen	malevolently	knell
amenities	subdued	emaciated	shroud
proprietor	disposition	temerity	snidely
concession	monotonous	reprimand	plantation

noncommittal	maverick	crescendo	boycott
languidly	flaunting	chiffonier	insolently
reverberated	adamantly	resiliency	feigned
lethargically	imperiously	moronic	impaled
admonished	interjected	flaccid	compassion

UNDERSTANDING THE SETTING

You may want to provide students with background information concerning the time and place of this book. Explain that the 1930s were a time of hardship for most people because of the Depression, but particularly so for African Americans at the bottom of the economic ladder in the South. Remind students that although the Fourteenth Amendment in 1868 recognized African Americans as United States citizens and the Fifteenth Amendment in 1870 gave African American men the right to vote, individual states still found many ways to discriminate against formerly enslaved people. Discuss what segregation meant at the time *Roll of Thunder, Hear My Cry* takes place.

GETTING STARTED

Use these suggestions to introduce the book to the class:

• Write the book title on the board, and invite students to suggest what they think it means. Have students record their ideas in literature notebooks so they can revisit the ideas after reading the book.

• Read aloud the dedication and the author's note at the beginning of the book. Point out that because enslaved people were rarely given the opportunity to learn to read and write, oral traditions and the art of storytelling have played an important role in African American history. Thus, not only are oral traditions entertaining, but they also provide a way to pass along ideas and information.

• Draw students' attention to examples of dialogue in the story, and discuss why it is written that way. Talk about the different kinds of accents that people in various parts of the United States may have.

TEACHER TIP

Have students locate Mississippi on a United States map and then find Vicksburg. Mention that Papa works in Louisiana. In what direction is that state from Vicksburg?

5

Exploring the Book

CHAPTERS 1 – 4

WHAT HAPPENS

The Logan children walk to school with other African American students while the white children ride a bus to their separate school. When the school bus splashes the Logan children on purpose one time too often, they dig a ditch so it will get stuck in the mud. Although their teacher is excited that this year the children will have books, Cassie's brother refuses to take his because it is old and torn, after having been used for 11 years by white students before being sent to the black school. Stacey and his friend T.J. have a falling out when T.J. cheats and Stacey gets punished for it. At home, the Logan children are surprised when their father, who has been working on a railroad to earn money, returns. With him is a large man, Mr. Morrison, who will stay and work on the family farm. The talk in the community is of a recent burning done by night riders; one man is dead and others are badly injured. That night the night riders are out again. The Logan children follow T.J. to the Wallace store where they have been forbidden to go because the Wallaces fleece the black sharecroppers and sell liquor to young people. After Stacey tells his mother what they've done, Mama begins organizing a boycott of the Wallace store.

QUESTIONS TO TALK ABOUT
COMPREHENSION AND RECALL

1. What does T.J. want Stacey to do about Mrs. Logan's tests? (*get the answers beforehand*)

2. Why does it take the Logans and their friends an hour to walk to school? (*Only white children have a bus; few provisions are made for educating black children.*)

3. What happens to the Berrys? (*White men set them on fire; John Henry dies.*)

4. Why doesn't Cassie like T.J? (*He's sneaky; cheats and gets Stacey in trouble.*)

5. Why does the Great Faith School start later and end earlier than the Jefferson Davis County School? (*Black children must work in the fields from early spring until October.*)

6. How do the Logan children get back at the bus driver? (*They dig a ditch which fills with rain; the bus breaks an axle.*)

7. Why does Stacey disobey Mama and go to the Wallace store? (*to get T.J. who got him in trouble*)

8. How do the landowners and storekeepers take advantage of the sharecroppers? (*Landowners sign to get credit for sharecroppers at store; store then charges huge interest on sharecropper purchases. When crops come in, landowners take half the profit, store gets paid back and charges fees for extending credit. Sharecropper never gets any cash and is always in debt.*)

9. Why is the land so important to the Logans? (*It represents freedom from being a sharecropper; a kind of pride and independence.*)

10. Why is Miss Crocker so pleased with the old, dirty books? (*It's the first time the school has had* any *books; she is probably used to being treated shabbily; she "knows her place."*)

11. Why does Miss Crocker say Mama is "biting the hand that feeds" her? (*Mama isn't grateful for the old books; she speaks of other things the school needs.*)

12. Why does Mr. Grimes, the bus driver, go out of his way to get the black children dirty? (*Possible: He's prejudiced; thinks it's funny.*)

13. Why does Stacey say he'll tell Mama what happened at the Wallace store? (*He knows it's the right thing to do; Mr. Morrison has let him make his own decision.*)

14. What problems do you predict for the Logans and others in the rest of the story? (*Answers will vary.*)

LITERARY ELEMENTS

15. Voice: Who is telling this story? (*Cassie*)

PERSONAL RESPONSE

16. How do you feel about the way black children were educated in the 1930s?

CROSS-CURRICULAR ACTIVITIES

LANGUAGE ARTS: *Storytelling*

Mildred Taylor writes that from the storytelling of her father: "... I learned to respect the past, to respect my own heritage and myself." Urge students to think of their own family stories and what they have learned from the stories. Then hold a class storytelling session. Students may also tell stories about themselves and their experiences that they would like to pass on. Sit in a circle, and invite volunteers to share their stories.

SOCIAL STUDIES: *Researching Reconstruction*

Assign research teams the task of reporting on historical subjects related to the book. For instance, one team might cover Reconstruction, another might research share-cropping, and a third group might find out about the Depression of the 1930s. Students may present their findings in a variety of ways such as a plan for a Web page, in the form of a documentary, as a segment of a television news magazine, or an article in a print magazine.

MATH: *Showing Interest*

The story provides an opportunity for a mini-lesson on interest. Teach students how interest is computed and compounded. Discuss both the positive aspect of interest that accumulates on capital and the negative aspect of high interest rates, penalties for failure to make payments, and the ways that a borrower can get in over his or her head. Be sure students understand that high interest was only part of the reason that sharecroppers were frequently mired in debt.

WHAT HAPPENS

When Cassie goes to Strawberry with Big Ma, she angers a white storekeeper by asking for service and a girl named Lillian Jean Simms by accidentally bumping into her. Cassie is shocked when Mr. Simms throws her off the sidewalk after the incident, and when Big Ma makes her

apologize to Lillian Jean. Mr. Morrison has to persuade Uncle Hammer not to take on Mr. Simms. Stacey gives his new coat, a gift from Uncle Hammer, to T.J. because it is too big and T.J. has been teasing him about it. Mama's boycott of the Wallace store gets underway with the help of a white lawyer, Mr. Jamison. Mr. Granger, the largest landowner in the region, threatens the Logans. His goal is to get their land, which his family once held. Cassie plans her revenge on Lillian Jean. T.J. cheats in school again, and Mama flunks him. In retaliation, he complains to the Wallaces about her teaching and she loses her job. The Logan children and other school children begin to boycott T.J.

QUESTIONS TO TALK ABOUT

COMPREHENSION AND RECALL

1. How does Mama want to retaliate for the burning of the Berry men? (*She wants people to boycott the Wallace store.*)

2. How does Mr. Granger threaten the Logans? (*He says they'll lose their land if they stir up trouble because the bank won't honor their mortgage. He also says the sharecroppers will get less for their cotton and won't be able to pay their debts.*)

3. How does Mr. Granger take his anger out on Mama? (*He gets her fired.*)

4. Why does Stacey drop T.J. as a friend? (*T.J. is responsible for getting Mama fired; T.J. speaks negatively of her because he failed her class.*)

HIGHER LEVEL THINKING SKILLS

5. Why does Big Ma take Cassie and Stacey to market? (*She has to take T.J. and doesn't want to put up with him alone.*)

6. Why doesn't Cassie understand Mr. Barnett's behavior? (*She sees that it is rude and unfair, but doesn't realize this is how African American people are usually treated.*)

7. Why does Big Ma make Cassie apologize to Lillian Jean? (*She's afraid of trouble and violence; she's protecting Cassie.*)

8. What kinds of arguments do you think Mr. Morrison used to persuade Uncle Hammer not to visit the Simms? (*Possible: You'll get hurt or killed; think about your brother; Mama and the children will get hurt. Wait, find another way to handle this. Turn the other cheek—there is more at stake here than Cassie's pride.*)

9. How would you describe Uncle Hammer? (*Possible: proud, angry, resentful, tough, impulsive, hot-headed, defiant, generous*)

10. Why does Cassie think Uncle Hammer's tongue-lashing is worse than her father's whipping? (*Uncle Hammer is very angry, gets cold look in his eye, shows his disgust with Stacey's stupidity. She's more sure of Papa's love and values.*)

11. Why will boycotting the Wallace store be dangerous? (*Harlan Granger owns the land the store is on and gets part of the income. It means pointing a finger and saying the Wallaces should be punished for burning and killing a black man.*)

LITERARY ELEMENTS

12. **Mood:** What is the mood of the story at the end of Chapter 7? (*ominous, dangerous, threatening, defiant*)

PERSONAL RESPONSE

13. How do you feel about the way Cassie handles her problem with Lillian Jean?

CROSS-CURRICULAR ACTIVITIES

SCIENCE: *King Cotton*
Remind students that the characters in the story depend on cotton as their main crop. In 1930 it took a farmer about 270 hours of work to produce one bale of cotton; today this process is much shorter. Have students find out about the cotton plant and how it is grown. You may want to divide the class into groups to report on the cotton plant, the uses of cotton and cottonseed, how cotton is grown, how it is harvested, where in the United States cotton is grown, and why it is grown in those regions.

WRITING: *What Is a Friend?*
Discuss the relationship between Stacey and T.J. in the story. Then ask students to write an essay describing what they think a good friend should be, and how Stacey and T.J. each stack up as a friend.

SOCIAL STUDIES: *Uncle Hammer's War*
Tell students that Uncle Hammer fought in World War I. Explain that when the United States entered this war in 1917, many African American men volunteered for the armed services. By joining the fight for liberty abroad, they hoped to encourage more liberty at home. Ask students to find out about the all-black units that fought

WHAT HAPPENS

Mr. Avery backs out of the boycott; Mr. Granger is putting pressure on the other sharecroppers, too. Papa takes Stacey to Vicksburg to buy groceries for the boycotters. An "accident" causes their wagon to roll over on Papa and break his leg so he's unable to return to his railroad job. The bank calls the mortgage on the Logans' land, and Uncle Hammer sells his car to raise money. At the revival, T.J. brags about his new friends the Simms boys. The Simms and T.J. later break into the Barnett's store. R.W. hits Mr. Barnett. When the Simms brothers hurt T.J. after the robbery, he comes to Stacey for help. That night the night riders show up at the Avery house. Mr. Jamison stops them, and the sheriff takes T.J. The mob turns threatening and wants to hang T.J. To avert the violence, Papa sets fire to the cotton fields. Soon everyone is fighting the fire and the hanging is momentarily forgotten. But when Mr. Barnett dies from his injuries. T.J.'s fate is sealed.

QUESTIONS TO TALK ABOUT

COMPREHENSION AND RECALL

1. Who kills Mr. Barnett? (*R.W. hits him with an ax.*)

2. How does Papa get Mr. Granger to stop the crowd at the Averys? (*He sets fire to the cotton.*)

HIGHER LEVEL THINKING SKILLS

3. In what ways are Mama and Papa brave? (*They are risking a lot—friendships, their land, their family's safety, their lives—to stand up to injustice.*)

4. Why does Papa defend Mr. Avery's and Mr. Lanier's decision to back out of the boycott? (*He understands what is at stake for them—being sent to a chain gang; they are sharecroppers and don't own any land.*)

5. Why does Papa think Stacey should go with him when he asks people about Vicksburg? (*He feels Stacey should be strong and learn how to handle himself.*)

6. How does Stacey grow up after the wagon accident? (*He feels responsible; tries to protect his brothers and sisters from harshness of story.*)

7. Why is the revival so important? (*It's a chance for people to get together, feast, reaffirm beliefs.*)

8. How does Uncle Hammer show that the land is important to him? (*He sells his car to raise money for the mortgage.*)

9. Why does T.J. believe the Simms brothers care about him? (*He isn't very bright; he wants to feel important; he thinks highly of himself.*)

LITERARY ELEMENTS

10. Character: Why does Stacey decide to help T.J. after the robbery at the Barnetts' store? (*He understands that T.J. is vulnerable and in real trouble. He feels responsible for T.J.'s safety; he's loyal.*)

11. Mood: How does the author create an ominous mood in Chapter 11? (*storm, thunder, lightning, heavy air*)

PERSONAL RESPONSE

12. What is your response to the story's ending?

CROSS-CURRICULAR ACTIVITIES

LANGUAGE ARTS: *Listen to the Language*
Draw students' attention to Mildred Taylor's use of language. Give the following as an example: "Papa stared out as a bolt of lightning splintered the sky into a dazzling brilliance." Ask students to note the author's use of verbs such as "splintered" and adjectives such as "dazzling." Encourage them to find other places in the story where the author's choice of words paints a vivid picture.

LITERATURE: *Best Books*
Talk about how scarce and prized books were in Cassie's childhood. If possible, have students look through copies of the books the Logan children get for Christmas: *The Count of Monte Cristo, The Three Musketeers,* and *Aesop's Fables.* Then ask them to select a favorite book for each of the four Logan children. Remind students to check the children's ages before they begin. Allow time for students to explain why they chose the books they did.

SOCIAL STUDIES: *Civil Rights*
Point out that things have changed since the 1930s in the area of civil rights. Have students use butcher paper to make a timeline from 1930 to the present showing some of the key events—and people—that have brought about these changes.

MUSIC: *Singing the Story*
Read aloud the song that begins Chapter 11 and from which the story gets its title. In many cases, songs were the only way enslaved people working in the fields could communicate with each other and voice their feelings. Ask students to find out more about early African American songs and hymns and to bring in examples to class. Suggest that they can do a visual presentation by illustrating a song's lyrics or an auditory presentation by playing a tape or CD recording or by singing the song.

Summarizing the Book

PUTTING IT ALL TOGETHER

Use one or more of the following activities to help students summarize and review *Roll of Thunder, Hear My Cry.*

CLASS PROJECT: *Story Roles*

Point out that not everyone in the book is completely good or completely bad. In fact, some of the characters are complex. On the board, make a chart such as the one shown below. Work with the class to complete it by discussing how each character fits or doesn't fit each of the headings of Hero, Villain, and Victim. You may add other characters. Students may also suggest other headings.

Character	Hero/ Heroine	Villain	Victim
Cassie			
Papa			
Mama			
Stacey			
T.J.			
Jeremy			
Mr. Jamison			
Big Ma			
Uncle Hammer			

GROUP PROJECT: *Literature Circles*

This book addresses many important issues which students can discuss in groups. Give each group one of the cards on page 16 to use as a discussion starter. Set rules for group discussion beforehand, and walk around to monitor students' progress. If desired, have the groups exchange cards so they can talk about more than one issue.

PARTNER PROJECT: *Chapter by Chapter*

As a summarizing project, have students work with partners to write a title for each of the book's 12 chapters. Explain that the titles should in some way reflect the events of the chapter. Some students may prefer to illustrate the chapters. Bring the class together to review and assess the different kinds of titles students write.

INDIVIDUAL PROJECT: *A Visual Response*

Invite students to show their responses to the book by creating collages. Suggest that they use a variety of materials to represent the people, events, and feelings of the story. Allow time for students to present their collages to the class. Set aside wall space for a showing of their work.

EVALUATION IDEAS

Ask the class to brainstorm a set of rubrics to use in assessing one of the summarizing projects. For example, a rubric for *Chapter by Chapter* might include the following objectives:

• Do the titles reflect the main event of each chapter?

• Do students include titles for all 12 chapters?

• Are the chapter titles written correctly?

• Do the titles capture the mood of the chapters?

Possible Answers for Worksheets

Page 14: 1. jealousy **2.** to humiliate; prove herself superior **3.** anger and revenge **4.** anger and indignation; loyalty to Little Man **5.** fear **6.** to help; bring about change; make amends for other whites' behavior **7.** to protect him from later trouble **8.** to stand up for what's right; make gesture after the Berry burnings **9.** wants acceptance and friendship **10.** wants to be respected, not ridiculed

Page 15: Answers will vary. Possible: **1.** You can't blame circumstances of birth. It isn't what happens to you; it's how you face it. **2.** Some people have no real self-esteem; instead they need to feel superior to others to feel they have any respect. **3.** You may have to take some things in order to make a stand for other things that are really important to you. **4.** You have to do what you believe is right; and not base your beliefs on what other people think.

Page 16: Students' discussions will vary.

Motives and Meaning

Why do the characters act the way they do? Sometimes they act on their feelings. At other times they have a purpose. Explain the motive of each character's actions for the event described.

Character	Action	Motive
1. T.J.	makes fun of Stacey's new coat	
2. Lillian Jean	wants Cassie to apologize for bumping into her	
3. Uncle Hammer	wants to go to the Simms after Cassie is pushed into the road	
4. Cassie	tells Miss Crocker she doesn't want the reading book	
5. Big Ma	makes Cassie apologize to Lillian Jean	
6. Mr. Jamison	offers to back the credit in Vicksburg	
7. Papa	cautions Stacey against Jeremy's friendship	
8. Mama	boycotts the Wallace store	
9. Jeremy	brings gifts at Christmas	
10. Stacey	gives his coat to T.J.	

Name: _____

Assessing Advice

In the story Mama and Papa give their children advice. Explain in your own words what each parent is saying.

1. Mama says: ". . . we have no choice of what color we're born or who our parents are or whether we're rich or poor. What we do have is some choice over what we make of our lives once we're here."

_____

_____

_____

2. Mama says: ". . . he's one of those people who has to believe that white people are better than black people to make himself feel big."

_____

_____

_____

3. Papa says: "There are things you can't back down on, things you gotta take a stand on. But it's up to you to decide what them things are."

_____

_____

_____

4. Papa says: "It keeps on blooming . . . knowing all the time it'll never get as big as them other trees. Just keeps on growing and doing what it gotta do. . . . It give up, it'll die."

_____

_____

_____

Name: _____

Literature Circle Cards

Cut apart these cards along the dotted lines. Then use them to start a discussion of *Roll of Thunder, Hear My Cry*. After you read the card, take time to think about the questions. Share your opinions with the rest of your group. You may find that your original opinions change—or that they grow even stronger!

Was T.J.'s fate due to circumstances of the time and place or due to his own character? What do you think would happen to T.J. today?

What does the title of the book mean? Why do you think the author chose it?

What is the role of nature in this story? Is it just part of the setting or does the author use it as a character?

What is the difference between respect and fear? Which characters act out of respect? Which characters act out of fear?

How does violence breed violence? Which characters use violence in the story? What is the difference between physical and emotional violence?

Based on what has happened in the story, what do you think happens to these characters next: Cassie, Jeremy, Mama, and Papa? What do you think happens to the land? the Great Faith School?